Pictorial Archive of
DECORATIVE AND ILLUSTRATIVE
MORTISED CUTS

551 Designs for Advertising and Other Uses

Edited by
Carol Belanger Grafton

Dover Publications, Inc.
New York

Published in Canada by General Publishing Company, Ltd., 30 Lesmill Road, Don Mills, Toronto, Ontario.
Published in the United Kingdom by Constable and Company, Ltd.

Pictorial Archive of Decorative and Illustrative Mortised Cuts: 551 Designs for Advertising and Other Uses is a new work, first published by Dover Publications, Inc., in 1983. The selection and arrangement of illustrations are by Carol Belanger Grafton. The research and Publisher's Note are by Joseph M. Cahn.

DOVER *Pictorial Archive* SERIES

Dover Publications, Inc., 31 East 2nd Street, Mineola, N.Y. 11501

Library of Congress Cataloging in Publication Data
Main entry under title:

Pictorial archive of decorative and illustrative mortised cuts.

(Dover pictorial archive series)
  1. Type ornaments.   2. Commercial art—History—19th century.   3. Printing—Specimens.
I. Grafton, Carol Belanger.   II. Title: Mortised cuts.   III. Series.
Z250.3.P48   1983   686.2'24   83-11601
ISBN 0-486-24540-3

PUBLISHER'S NOTE

The joining of words and pictures in advertising art is nowhere more intimate than in mortised cuts. This printer's term refers to designs, usually pictorial, engraved on wood or stereotyped in metal from wood blocks, with one or more holes sawn into the plates so type could be inserted. Less strictly, it applies to the images printed from such cuts. In some nineteenth-century specimen books, the word "pierced" is used as a synonym for "mortised."

These cuts, perhaps more than any other genre of advertising art, convey a period feeling so distinctive that they are among the most sought-after graphic elements from nineteenth-century sources. For all their popularity, both then and now, these cuts are widely scattered through files of old periodicals and typefounders' and engravers' catalogues. The present collection represents an extensive search through rare printed materials too numerous to list here.

Artist Carol Belanger Grafton has selected 551 of the most interesting and versatile images and arranged them in categories. Anyone who has tried to find a vaguely remembered cut in one of the old specimen books, in which cuts were usually arranged haphazardly, will appreciate this organization, especially considering the sheer number of designs contained in this book. It is probably the largest and most varied compendium exclusively devoted to this genre of wood-engraving available today. Even the encyclopedic *Handbook of Early Advertising Art* edited by Clarence P. Hornung (Dover, 1947; Typographical Volume, 20123-6; Pictorial Volume, 20122-8)—that master swipe-file beloved of art directors and others in the graphics field—has less than half as many mortised cuts as the present volume.

Because this book was assembled for ready use as part of the Dover Pictorial Archive Series, rather than as an historical survey of advertising art, the original type has been removed from each cut. Today's users can simply set their own message to fit the space and paste it into position for offset reproduction, a far easier and less costly process than it was when printers purchased stock cuts (which often cost as much as $5.00 each in the 1870s and 80s) and fitted the type into the mortises, or had engravings made to order and then adapted for insertion of metal type.

In their most typical form, mortised cuts depict human figures holding scrolls, placards, sandwich boards, newspapers or some other writing surface. As message-bearers, these designs have much of the attention-getting power of their real-life models: the heralds, criers, "sandwich-men" and other precursors of the "talking heads" of the video age. The charm of the illustrations and the cunning with which slogans were embedded in them gave mortised cuts special impact and eye-appeal, particularly in the monotonous, largely typographical advertising pages of Victorian newspapers and magazines. Their appeal is still strong today.

Animals, especially beasts of burden draped with saddle-cloths, were also favorite subjects for mortised cuts. Floral compositions, landscape vignettes and other natural forms figure in this collection as well. The flat surfaces of boxes, barrels, drums and watches made suitable subjects for mortised cuts. Labels on bottles, cans and other packaged goods also served this purpose.

The range of illustration styles in this treasury is impressively broad. There are naively rendered designs in the manner of the early nineteenth century; silhouettes; cuts in the chapbook style; marvelously detailed and modeled figures from the golden age of wood-engraving; Art Nouveau style plates; and more—all with spaces for messages. There is an appealing variety of moods from which to choose. What could be more dignified than the classically draped female figure on page 42? (Her scroll originally proclaimed the efficacy of a much-publicized brand of cure-all pills.) For comic effect, there is the man on page 8 reading a newspaper in a rocker that is about to topple over, his arms and legs spread wide in a slapstick pose. There is also an entire section devoted to clowns and jesters. There are many sentimental images of children with a distinctively Victorian look of innocence. At the other extreme, there are cuts of sinister aspect: the Mephistophelean figure on page 10 holding a small sign that practically begs to be filled with an ominous warning is but one example.

The cutaway space can dominate the image so much that there is hardly any picture left, as in the cut at the top left of page 3. The protruding peaked hat and boots draw the reader's eye to the message that the rectangle contained. On the other hand the mortised area can be tiny relative to the design as a whole. Such cuts can serve as spot illustrations with a special power to communicate both verbally and pictorially.

Most of the designs in this book are the creations of anonymous artists employed by publishers or type-founding houses. However, there are among them a number of images drawn by Thomas Nast (1840–1902), the great American caricaturist and political cartoonist, who very often used graphic devices similar to mortised cuts. His small cartoons, which appeared in the back pages of *Harper's Weekly* during the 1860s and 70s, frequently relied on signboards and the like draped over the necks of the public figures being lampooned to tell part of the story. While these images are not mortised cuts in the strict technical sense (the lettering was usually done by hand and engraved in the same way as the pictorial background, rather than being set in type and mortised into position), these designs have a basic kinship to the stock cuts that were so familiar to Nast's readers in the nineteenth century.

The potential uses of the material in this book are virtually unlimited: advertising, packaging, posters, catalogues, circulars, and so on. Crisply reproduced in line, the images are ready to be cut out and filled in. Best of all, they are all copyright-free.

CONTENTS

2 Men

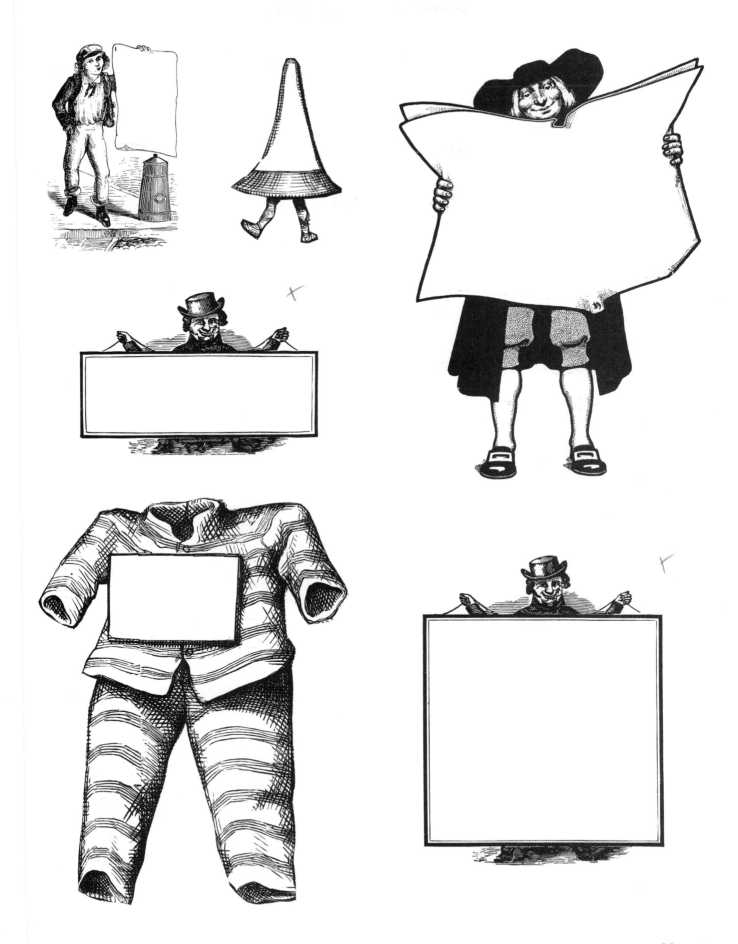

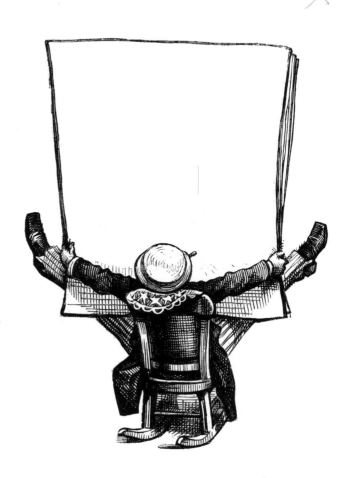

16 Men

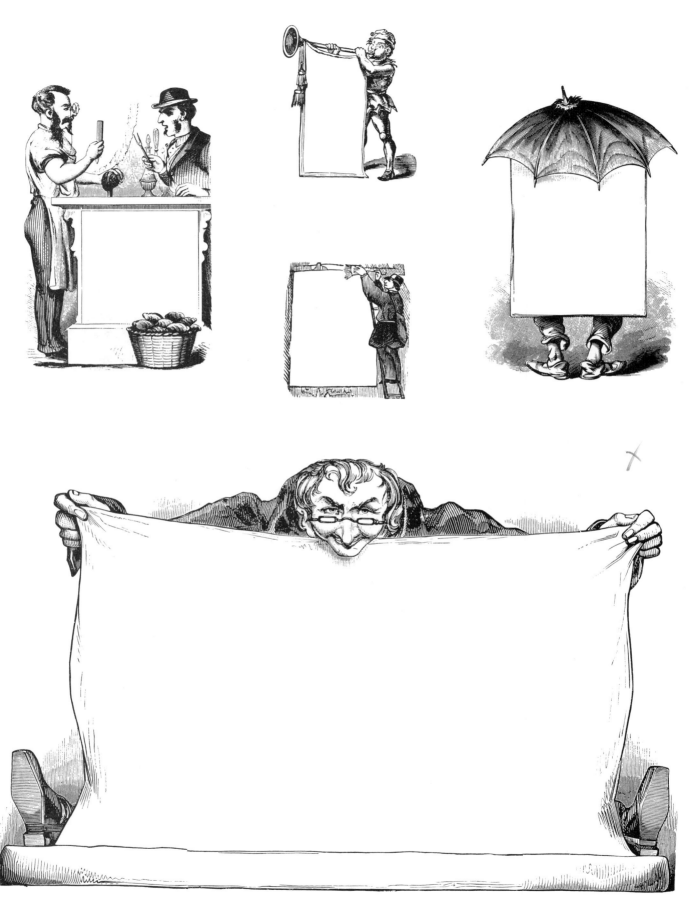

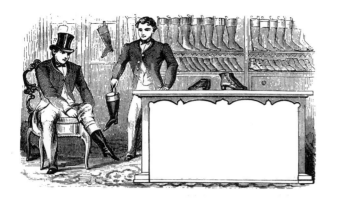

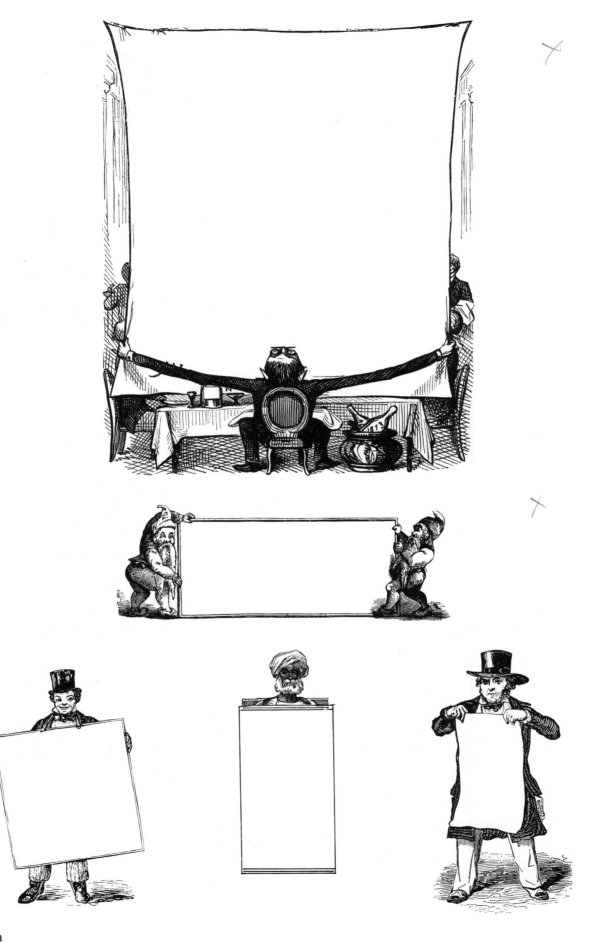

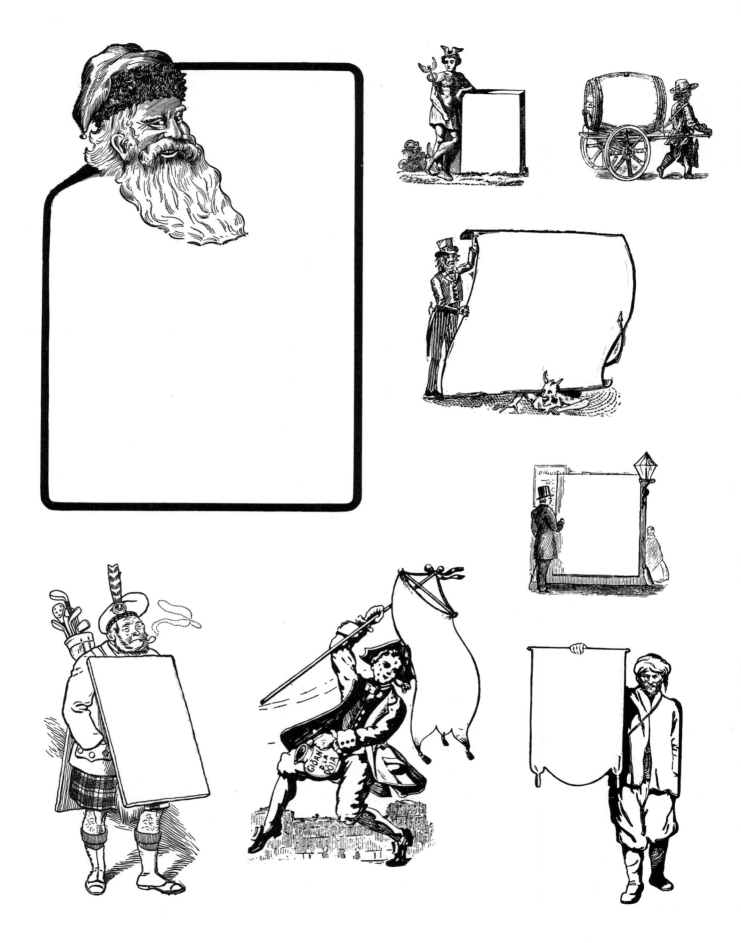

ELECTROPATH
BELT

HAMS

OIL

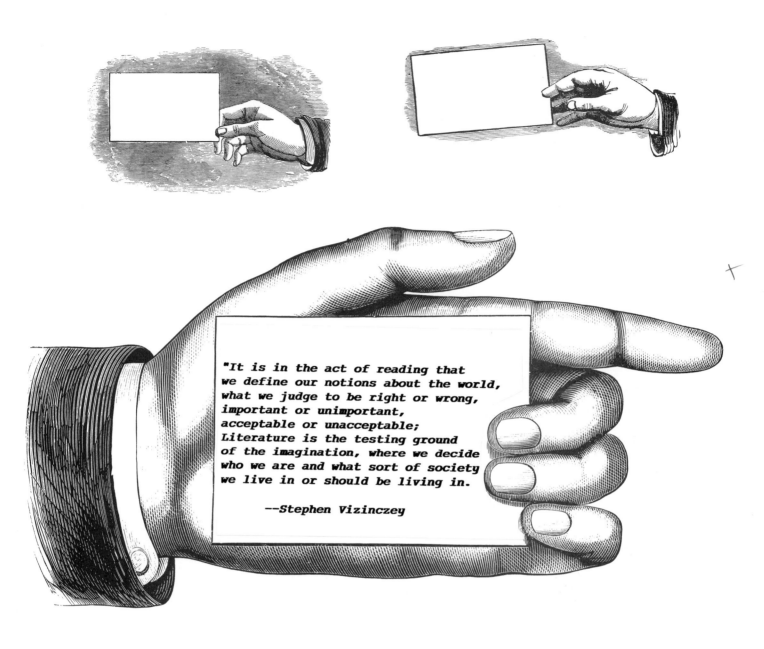

"It is in the act of reading that
we define our notions about the world,
what we judge to be right or wrong,
important or unimportant,
acceptable or unacceptable;
Literature is the testing ground
of the imagination, where we decide
who we are and what sort of society
we live in or should be living in.

--Stephen Vizinczey

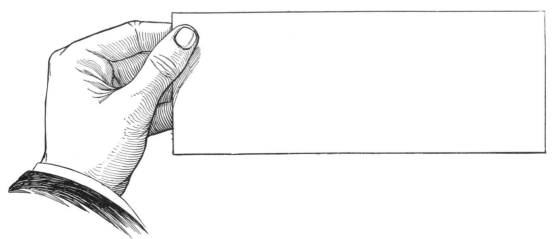

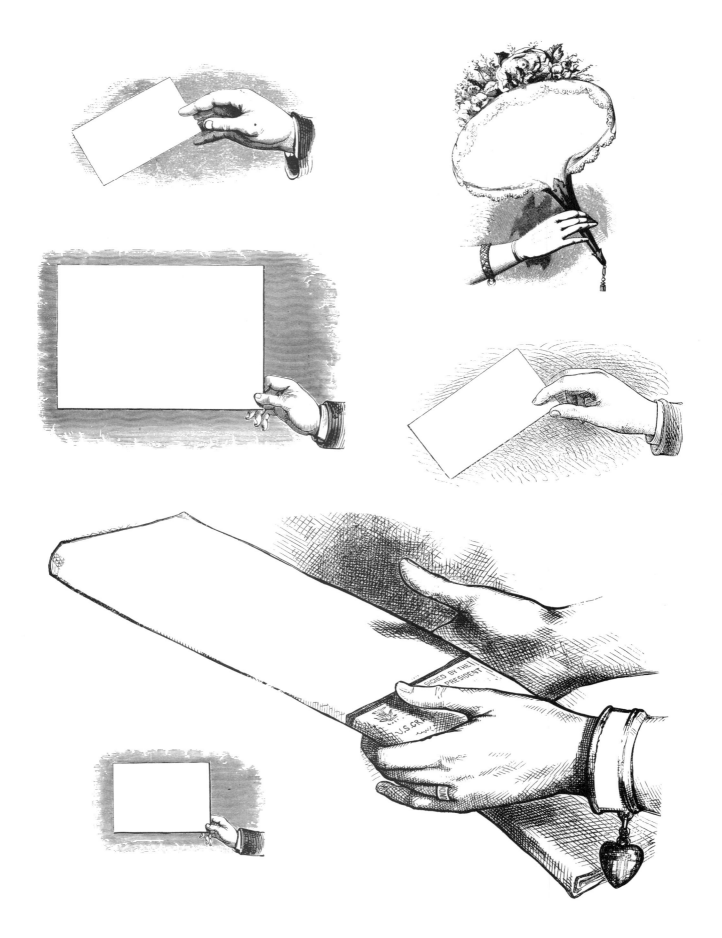

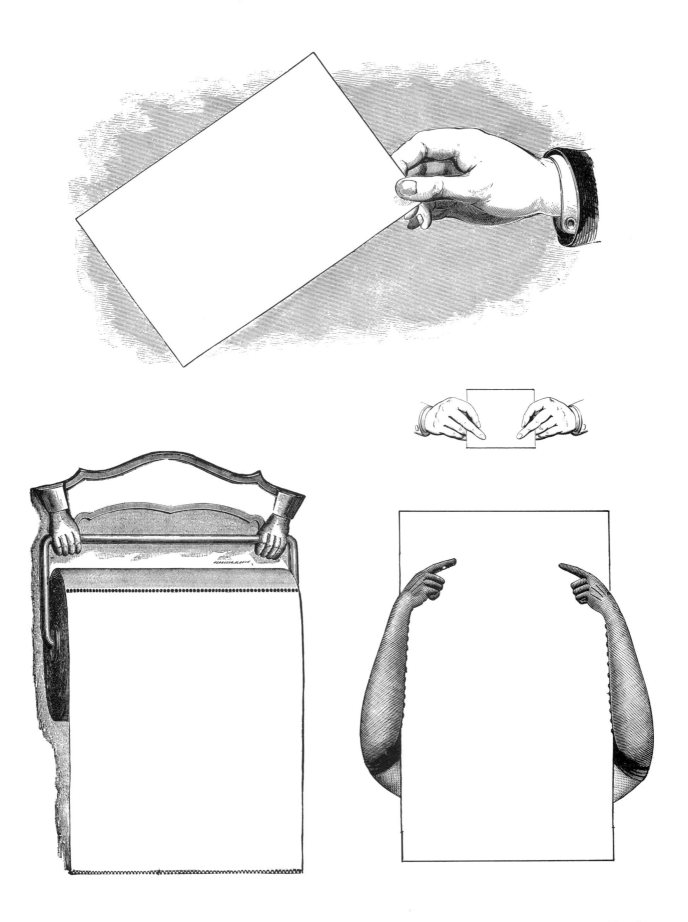

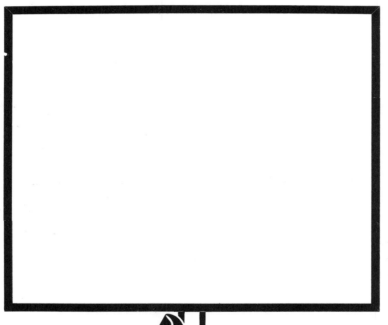

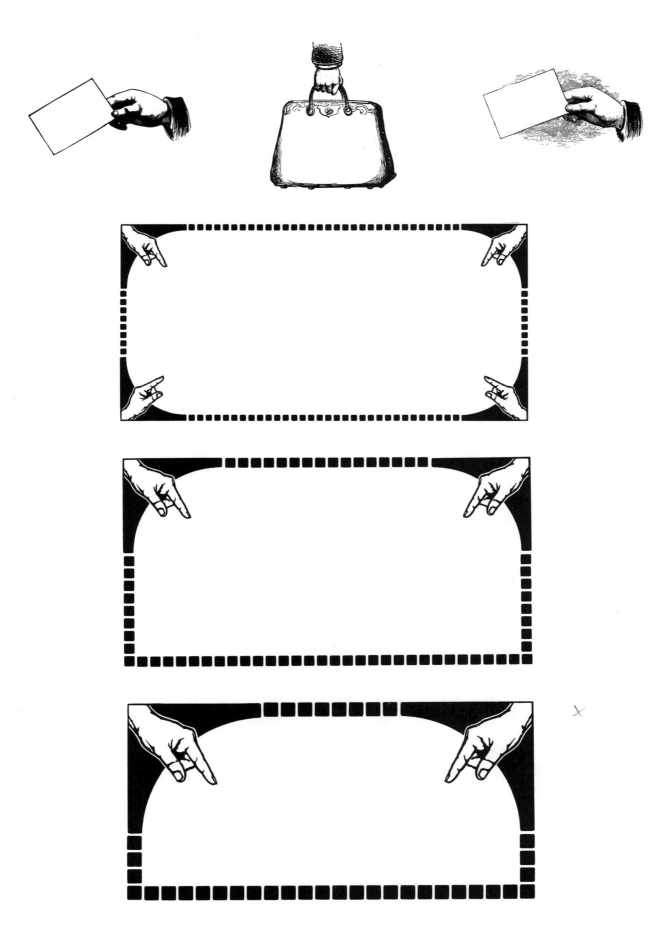

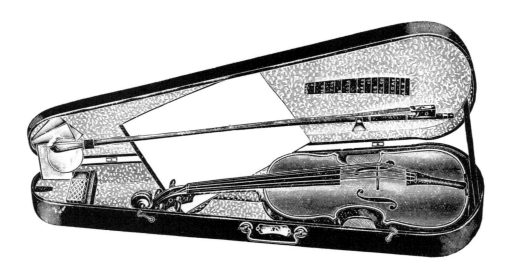

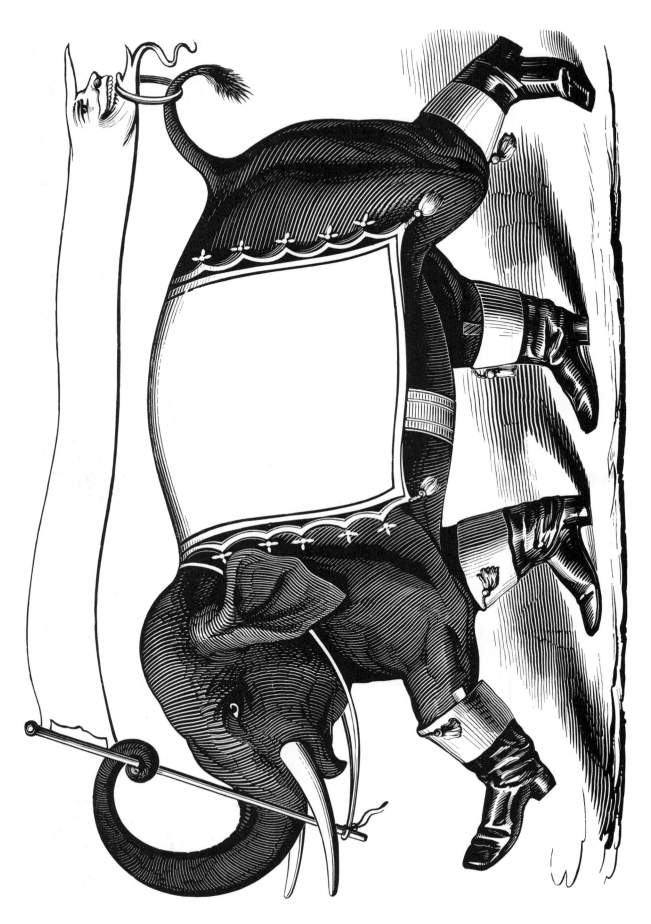

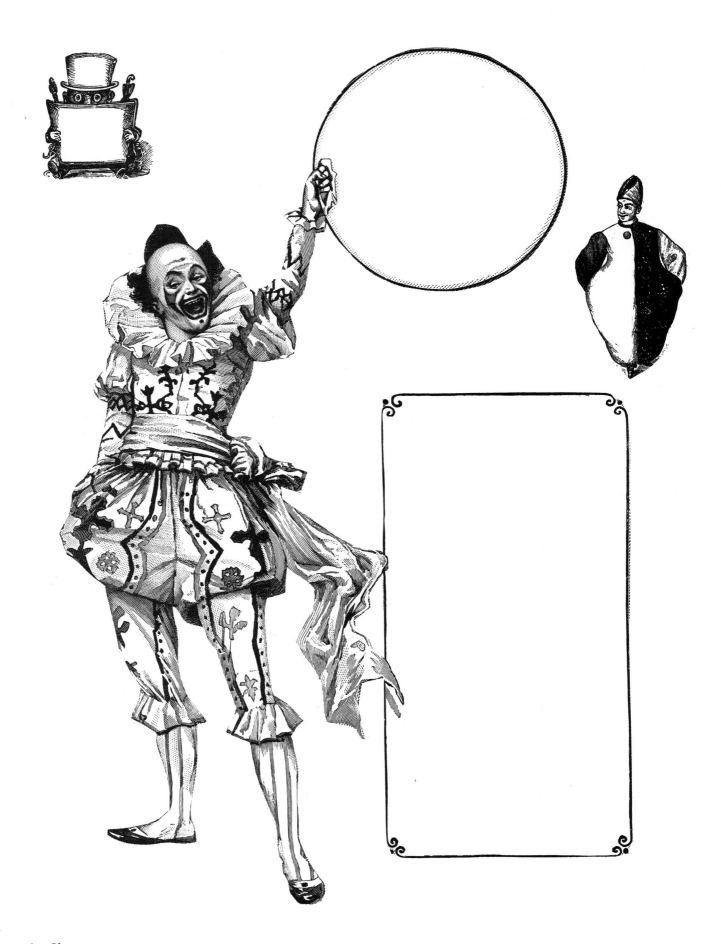

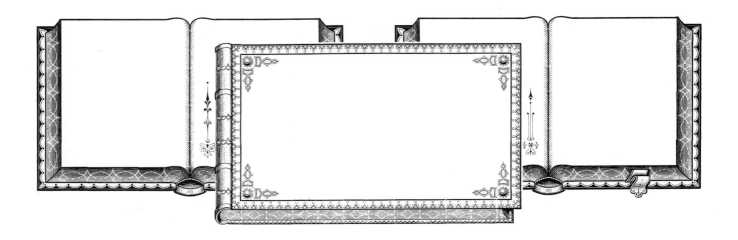

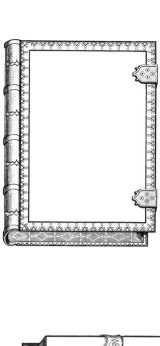

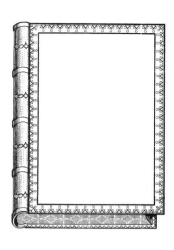

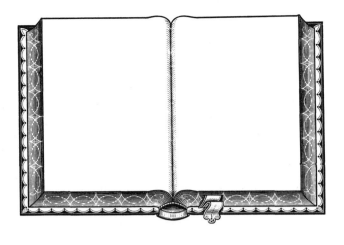

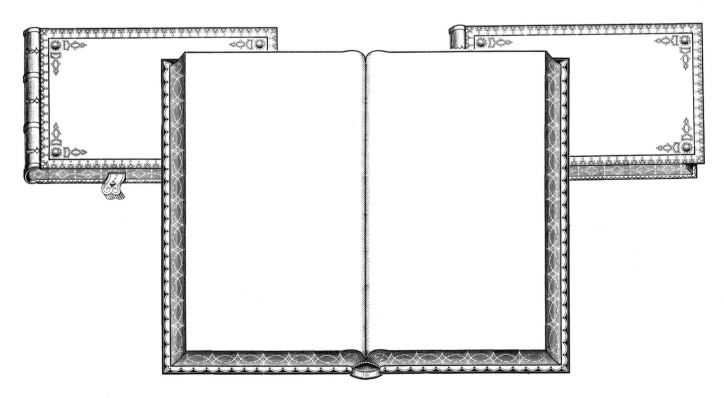

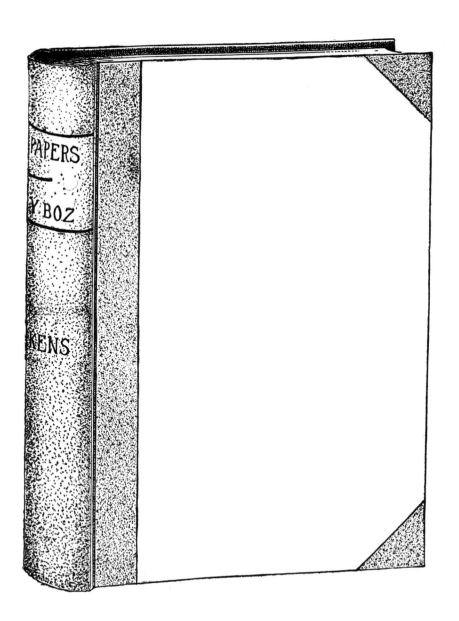

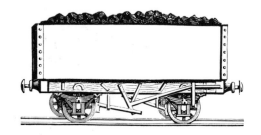

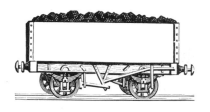

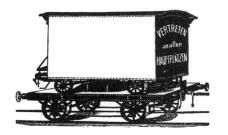

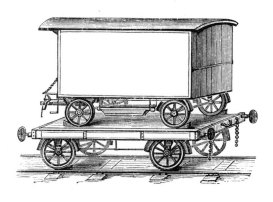

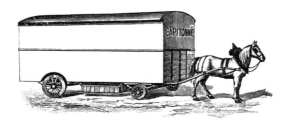

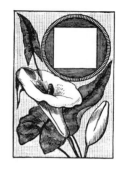

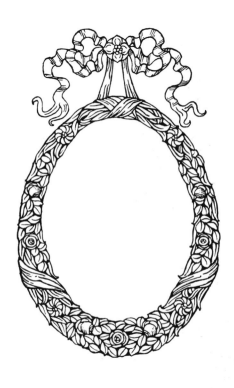

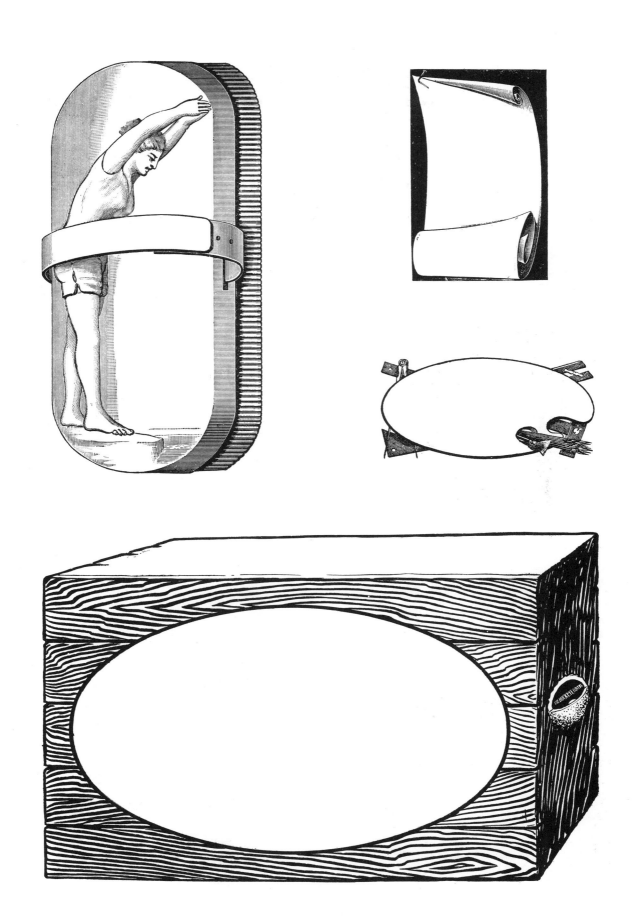

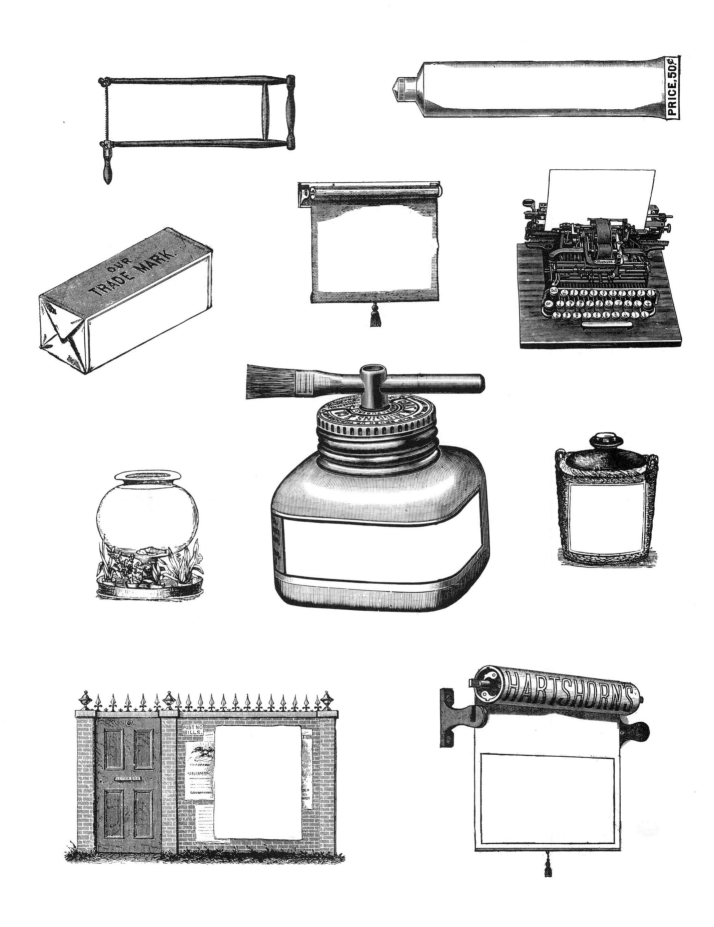

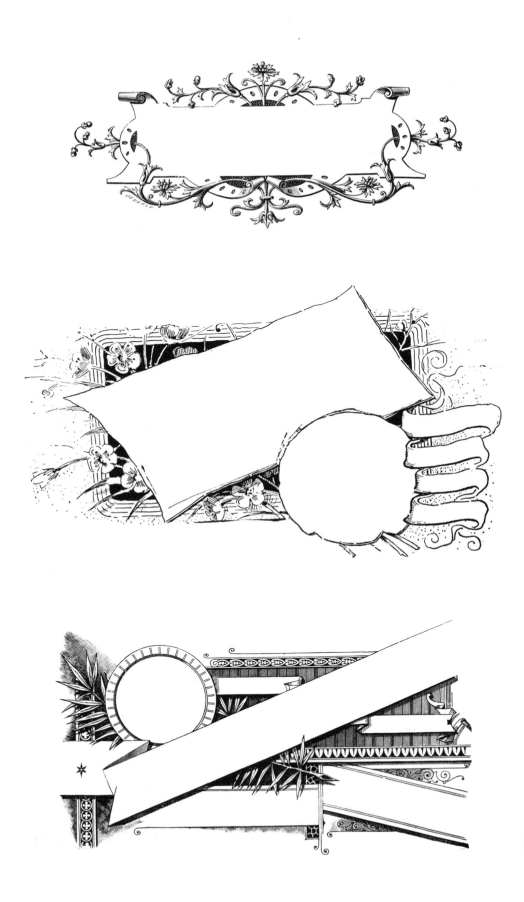